Marriage
The Mystery of Faithful Love

WORKS BY DIETRICH VON HILDEBRAND

IN ENGLISH
Liturgy and Personality†
Transformation in Christ
Jaws of Death: Gate of Heaven†
Marriage: The Mystery of Faithful Love†
In Defense of Purity
Fundamental Moral Attitudes
Ethics
The New Tower of Babel†
Situation Ethics
Graven Images
What is Philosophy?
Not as the World Gives
Man and Woman†
The Heart
The Art of Living†
The Trojan Horse in the City of God†
The Devastated Vineyard
Celibacy and the Crisis of Faith
The Encyclical *Humanae Vitae*
Satan at Work

IN GERMAN
Die Idee der sittlichen Handlung
Sittlichkeit und ethische Werterkenntnis
Metaphysik der Gemeinschaft
Das katholische Berufsethos
Engelbert Dollfuss: Ein katholischer Staatsmann
Zeitliches im Lichte des Ewigen
Der Sinn philosophischen Fragens und Erkennens
Die Menschheit am Scheideweg
Mozart, Beethoven, Schubert
Heiligkeit und Tüchtigkeit
Das Wesen der Liebe
Die Dankbarkeit
Ästhetik I & II
Moralia

†Available from Sophia Institute Press

Dietrich
von Hildebrand

Marriage
The Mystery of Faithful Love

SOPHIA INSTITUTE PRESS

Manchester, New Hampshire

Marriage was first published in German in 1929 as *Die Ehe*. Longmans, Green, and Co. published the first English translation in 1942. In 1984, Sophia Institute Press published a paperback edition (retitled *Marriage: The Mystery of Faithful Love*) and in 1991, a hardcover edition that added subtitles and was slightly revised to perfect the translation. This 1997 paperback edition duplicates the 1991 edition.

The cover painting is a detail from *The Holy Family* (Doni Tondo) by Michelangelo Buonarroti, in the Uffizi, Florence, Italy (photo courtesy of Nicolo Orsi Battaglini/Art Resource, New York).

Sophia Institute Press
Box 5284, Manchester, NH 03108
1-800-888-9344

Nihil obstat: Arthur J. Scanlan, S.T.D., *Censor Librorum*
Imprimatur: Francis J. Spellman, D.D., Archbishop, N.Y.
February 27, 1942

Library of Congress Cataloging-in-Publication Data
Von Hildebrand, Dietrich, 1889-1977
    [*Ehe*. English]
    Marriage : the mystery of faithful love / Dietrich von Hildebrand.
        p. cm.
    Translation of: *Die Ehe*.
    ISBN 0-918477-11-5 (hdbk.) — ISBN 0-918477-00-X (pbk. : alk. paper)
    1. Marriage. 2. Marriage–Religious aspects–Catholic Church.
    3. Love. I. Title.
HQ739.V6I3 1991   306.81 — dc20   91-36153

97 98 99 00 01 10 9 8 7 6 5 4 3 2

Table of Contents

Introduction

by Alice von Hildebrand

"LOVE IS HEAVEN; marriage is Hell," wrote Lord Byron 150 years ago. At the time, he could not have foreseen the incredible popularity that his idea would have today.

In our society, the beauty and greatness of married love has been so obscured that most people now view marriage as a prison: a conventional, boring, legal matter that threatens love and destroys freedom.

My husband, Dietrich von Hildebrand, was just the opposite. Long before he converted to Roman Catholicism, he was convinced that the community of love in marriage is one of the deepest sources of human happiness.

He saw the grandeur and the beauty of the union of spouses in marriage — symbolized by their physical union which leads in such a mysterious way to the creation of a new human person. He recognized that love by its very essence longs for infinity and for eternity. Therefore, a person truly in love wants to bind himself forever to his beloved — which is precisely the gift that marriage gives him.

In contrast, love without an unqualified commitment betrays the very essence of love. He who refuses to commit himself (or who breaks a commitment in order to start another relationship) fools himself. He confuses the excitement of novelty with authentic happiness.

Such affective defeatism — so typical of our age — is a symptom of a severe emotional immaturity which weakens the very foundation of society. It is rooted partly in a misunderstanding of freedom. Many people criticize marriage because they fail to realize that a person also exercises his freedom when he freely binds himself to another in marriage.

These critics of marriage do not see that continuity — and especially faithfulness — is an essential characteristic of a truly great personality: he chooses to remain faithful to what he has seen, even though his vision may later become blurred.

In matters of love and marriage, "Hell" does not come from *fidelity*; it comes from *lack of fidelity*, which leaves men technically *un*bound but actually solitary: trapped in a shallow arbitrariness and a stifling subjectivism.

Introduction

Indeed, contrary to Lord Byron and to popular belief, marriage is the friend and protector of love between man and woman. Marriage gives love the structure, the shelteredness, the climate in which alone it can grow.

Marriage teaches spouses humility and makes them realize that the human person is a very poor lover. Much as we long to love and to be loved, we repeatedly fall short and desperately need help. We must bind ourselves through sacred vows so that the bond will grant our love the strength necessary to face the tempest-tossed sea of our human condition.

For no love is free from periods of difficulties. But (as Kierkegaard aptly remarks), because it implies will, commitment, duty, and responsibility, marriage braces spouses to fight to save the precious gift of their love. It gives them the glorious confidence that with God's help, they will overcome the difficulties and emerge victorious. Thus, by adding a formal element to the material element of love, marriage guarantees the future of love and protects it against the temptations which are bound to arise in human existence.

In a relationship without commitment, the slightest obstacle, the most insignificant difficulty, is a legitimate excuse for separating. Unfortunately, man — who is

Marriage

usually so eager to win a fight over others — shows little or no desire to conquer himself. It is much easier for him to give up a relationship than to fight what Kierkegaard calls "the lassitude which often is wont to follow upon a wish fulfilled."

Marriage calls each spouse to fight against himself for the sake of his beloved. This is why it has become so unpopular today. People are no longer willing to achieve the greatest of all victories, the victory over self.

To abolish marriage is, as Kierkegaard tells us, "self-indulgence." Only cowards malign marriage. They run from battle, defeated before the struggle even begins. Marriage alone can save love between man and woman and place it above the contingencies of daily flux and moods. Without this bond, there is no reason to wish to transform the dreariness of everyday life into a poetic song.

Sacramental marriage

In *Marriage: The Mystery of Faithful Love*, my husband introduced these themes which illuminate the value and importance of natural marriage and show the role that marriage plays in serving faithful love.

At the same time, my husband saw that even in the happiest of natural marriages, mortal man — the creature of a day (as Plato calls him) — remains terribly finite and limited. Consequently, every merely natural love is necessarily tragic: it will never achieve the eternal union for which it naturally longs.

But when my husband converted to Catholicism, he discovered a wonderful new dimension of marriage: its sacramental character as a fountain of grace. St. Paul illuminated the sublime dignity of sacramental marriage in calling it a "great mystery," comparable to the love of Christ for His Church.[1] Natural love pales in comparison to the beauty of a love rooted in Christ.

As a Sacrament, marriage gives people the supernatural strength necessary to "fight the good fight."[2] Every victory achieved together over habit, routine, and boredom cements the bonds existing between the spouses and makes their love produce new blossoms.

Also, because it explicitly and sacramentally unites the spouses with the infinite love that Christ has for each one of them, sacramental marriage overcomes the

[1] Eph. 5:32

[2] 1 Tim. 6:12

tragic limits of natural marriage and achieves the infinite and eternal character to which every love aspires.

It is therefore understandable that after his conversion to Roman Catholicism, my husband (who was already the great knight for natural love) became an ardent knight in defense of the supernatural love found in sacramental marriage. His enthusiasm for the great beauty and mystery of faithful love in marriage led to the writing of this work.

History of this book

The preparation of *Marriage* actually began in 1923 when my husband gave a lecture on marriage at a Congress of the Catholic Academic Association in Ulm, Germany. The lecture was a resounding success.

In the lecture he argued that one should distinguish between the *meaning* of marriage (i.e., love) and its *purpose* (i.e., procreation). He portrayed marriage as a community of love, which, according to an admirable divine economy, finds its end in procreation.

Even though official Catholic teaching had until then put an almost exclusive stress on the importance of procreation as the purpose of marriage, the *practice* of the Church had always implicitly recognized love as the meaning of marriage. She had always approved the marriage of those who, because of age or other impediments, could not enjoy the blessings of children.

But conscious that he was breaking new ground in making so explicit the distinction between the *purpose* and the *meaning* of marriage, my husband sought the approval of Church authority. So he turned to His Eminence Cardinal Pacelli, then the Papal Nuncio in Munich.

To this future pope (Pius XII), my husband expounded his views and, to his joy, received from him a full endorsement of his position.

Cardinal Pacelli's approval coupled with the success of the lecture on marriage encouraged my husband to expand and develop the lecture into the small volume which you now have in your hands.

Since its first publication in German, *Marriage* has been translated into most of the major languages of Europe, where it has never lost popularity. When it was first translated into English during World War II, critics received it very favorably and the book enjoyed great popularity, remaining in print through four editions over fourteen years.

Marriage

It gives me great joy to greet this new edition, which once again makes *Marriage* available to English-speaking readers after an absence of nearly thirty years.

Especially today, this book — revealing the sublime Christian vocation of marriage — is a *must* for anyone who is anxious to live worthily this great mystery of love.

Thomas à Kempis tells us that "love is a great thing." So is marriage.

Foreword

by John Cardinal O'Connor

IN A WORLD in which marriage is frequently imperiled and denigrated in so many ways, it is imperative that the Church continually and faithfully announce the *good news* of marriage. This *good news* is solidly grounded in the central mysteries of our Faith.

Both the Old Testament and the New Testament graphically present the concept that marriage is analogous to the covenant between God and Israel and between Christ and His Church. The Scriptures clearly teach that the sacred commitment of marriage is intended by God to be the sacramental sign of His love for His people. It is revealed and traditionally understood that through the institution of marriage, God wishes to reveal to His people the scope and magnitude of His love for them.

This profound, long-standing theological concept was recently reaffirmed at the 1980 Synod of Bishops meeting in Rome. The Bishops unanimously state, "It is no wonder that throughout the history of salvation the marriage covenant has been understood and explained both in light of the covenant between God the Creator and the people of Israel and in light of the covenant between Christ and His bride, the Church. This relationship of love is not merely symbolic or allegorical but an ontological reality made manifest by the Incarnation through which all flesh was redeemed and made holy by Christ."

In *Familiaris Consortio*, his *Apostolic Exhortation on the Family*, Pope John Paul II states: "The communion of love between God and His people, a fundamental part of the revelation and faith experience of Israel, finds a meaningful expression in the marriage covenant which is established between a man and a woman. Their bond of love becomes the image and symbol of the covenant uniting God with His people."[3]

Marriage as a Sacrament, then, becomes the concrete, earthly expression and incarnation of God's saving love for each of us. Herein lies the essence of the sacramentality of marriage: through the loving marital

---

[3] *Familiaris Consortio*, Art. 12

relationship, God continues to make known His presence in the world.

In effect, when marital love and commitment that is open to life is expressed, God continues to take on flesh. God's love, therefore, does not simply transcend our own flesh, but rather comes and dwells in our midst. For a Christian, then, the vision of marriage must be rooted in one's commitment to Jesus and faith in Him as Lord.

Jesus announced the advent of His Kingdom as one of tenderness and intimacy. He speaks of a God whose love, mercy, and forgiveness is extravagant, limitless, and without reservation. He is a God of concern who is totally and permanently faithful in bringing Creation to fulfillment by constantly drawing us back to Himself, the source of all goodness. Since marriage is the living, tangible, sacramental sign of this love, these characteristics are to be expressed and experienced in the marital relationship.

You have been chosen and called, therefore, as husbands and wives to be for one another the living experiential sign and expression of God's love by sharing with each other the gifts of uncompromising love, unconditional acceptance, ceaseless dedication, total fidelity, and untiring service. These are the signs of God's love, and this is what makes God present in the Sacrament of Matrimony.

Such concepts are but a few among many which are beautifully articulated by the late Dietrich von Hildebrand in this book, *Marriage*.

I am certain that innumerable readers will share my joy that some forty years after its initial publication, and some twenty-eight years after it went out of print in English, *Marriage* has been reprinted. If anything, this beautiful essay is more critically needed today than it was forty years ago.

It is modern in the best sense of the term, the sense of Chesterton's reminder that the wonderful thing about Christianity is not that it is nineteen-hundred years old, but that it is nineteen-hundred years new.

Preface
by Dietrich von Hildebrand

OUR EPOCH is characterized by a terrible anti-personalism, a progressive blindness toward the nature and dignity of the spiritual person. This anti-personalism expresses itself mainly in a radical collectivism and in the different kinds of materialism. Of these, biological materialism is perhaps the most dangerous, for it considers man as a more highly developed animal, his whole personality determined by mere physiological elements. Human life is considered exclusively from a biological point of view and biological principles are the measure by which all human activities are judged.

In such an ideological situation, it seems very important to stress again the spiritual significance of marriage — and to explain not only its primary end (procreation), but also its primary meaning as the intimate union of two persons in mutual love.

"Magna res est amor!" — "A great thing is love!" Although directly referring to the love of God, this

saying of Blessed Thomas à Kempis can be applied to all authentic love and especially to conjugal love. An understanding of this is beginning to grow in different countries, and moral theologians are emphasizing the role of love in marriage, a role which was previously underestimated by some. In stressing the primary *end* of marriage — procreation — certain theological treatises have overlooked the primary *meaning* of marriage, which is love. The movement inspired by Abbé Violet in France has greatly contributed to a deeper understanding of marriage, through different important publications, congresses, and retreats for married couples. Many important books published in Germany reveal a similar development. The English works of Father John Martindale, S.J., and of Father T. G. Wayne, O.P., also set forth a conception of marriage not exclusively dominated by the point of view of procreation. Above all, the encyclical of Pope Pius XI, *De Casti Connubii*, refers to a passage of the Roman Catechism in which conjugal love is considered as the ultimate meaning of marriage.

This present work was written originally in German before the establishment of the above-mentioned movements, which were aimed at a deeper examination of the meaning of Christian marriage. And it is perhaps permissible to say that its influence, especially in its Italian and French translations, has been credited with bringing about an increased stress on the role of love in Christian marriage.

Unlike my book *In Defense of Purity*, this work is exclusively concerned with marriage and is addressed to a general public. Should the book in its English form contribute to a deeper awareness of the height, depth, and breadth of marriage concluded in Christ — that "great mystery in Christ"[4] according to the words of the Apostle — its purpose will be fulfilled.

I want to express my deep gratitude to my friends Dr. Emmanuel Chapman and Mr. Daniel Sullivan for all their help in the translation of this little book.

---

[4] Eph. 5:32

Love and marriage

Husbands, love your wives as
Christ loved the Church.
— St. Paul

THE GREATNESS and sublimity of marriage, the closest and most ultimate of unions, raised by Christ to the dignity of a Sacrament, is revealed at one stroke in the exhortation of St. Paul wherein he compares married love to the love of Christ, the Word made Flesh, for His Holy Church.[5]

The greatness of marriage

No natural human good has been exalted so high in the New Testament. No other good has been chosen to become one of the seven Sacraments. No other has been endowed with the honor of participating directly in the establishment of the Kingdom of God. This in itself suggests the infinitely precious value already attached to marriage in the realm of nature, the richness and grandeur it unfolds. Before we examine the nature,

[5] Eph. 5:25-27

the meaning, and the beauty of Christian marriage (which St. Paul calls "a great mystery in Christ and the Holy Church"[6]), we shall examine the essence and meaning of marriage in the realm of nature, and its specific character in reference to all other fellowships and communities.

Only in this way can we understand what was so gloriously exalted by Jesus Christ and thus dispel the misinterpretations of the nature of marriage so frequently encountered.

Several passages of Holy Scripture dignify marriage by employing it as an image of the relation between God and the soul. This relation prefigures in an imperfect fashion the perfect model, very much as the Old Testament prefigures the New. Indeed, Christ calls Himself *the spouse of the soul*, and the Song of Songs presents the union of Christ and the soul in the form of a betrothal.

Love is the core of marriage

Why does Holy Scripture choose this particular relationship as an image? It is chosen because marriage is the

[6] Eph. 5:32

closest and most intimate of all earthly unions in which, more than in any other, one person gives himself to another without reserve, where the other in his complete personality is the object of love, and where mutual love is in a specific way the theme (that is to say, the core) of the relationship.

Love is also the inmost core of the relation of the soul to God. Unquestionably, we owe adoration and obedience to the eternal King of Glory, the splendor of Everlasting Light. He is our Lord. Our duty here on earth is to serve Him in all things without reserve. Yet, three times He asks St. Peter, "Lovest thou me?"[7] Does not the chief Commandment which contains all the Law and the Prophets say, "Thou shalt love the Lord thy God with thy whole heart, with thy whole soul, with thy whole strength, and with thy whole mind"?[8]

Marriage has been chosen as the image of the perfect union between the soul and Christ because in marriage, likewise, the center and core is love. No other earthly community is constituted so exclusively in its very substance by mutual love.

[7] John 21:15
[8] Mark 12:30

5

Marriage

In friendship, for example, community of thought or spiritual interests and common experiences play a capital part. In the relationship between parent and child, the care and upbringing of their charges holds an essential place. At the root of the child's relationship to the parent is gratitude and obedience due for protection and care.

Of course, family relations, too, can be transfigured only by love, and should be permeated by love. But even though they can only unfold their real meaning on the basis of love and under its banner, the essence and exclusive principle of such relationships is not mutual love.

Subjectively considered, love does not enter so exclusively into the essence of their relations as it does in the case of marriage. Their objective character is not founded in the same way on love nor are they constituted to the same extent for love.

On the other hand, in marriage the fundamental subjective attitude and the objective *raison d'être* of the relationship, a relationship which also mysteriously serves to procreate new human beings, is mutual love.

Marriage is the wonderful union of two persons in love and by love. Later we shall see that in sacramental marriage this love is elevated to a mysterious communion of love and life in and for Christ. But this presupposes a unique mutual love, and it is in just this that the married couple glorifies Jesus Christ.

Love is the primary *meaning* of marriage just as the birth of new human beings is its primary *end*. The social function of marriage and its importance for the State are something secondary and subordinate. We shall understand this better if, putting aside for the moment the sacramental dignity of marriage and considering it simply as a natural communion, we recall the specific characteristics of conjugal love.

The characteristics of conjugal love

A widespread error, even in Catholic circles, holds that conjugal love is distinguished from love of friends or love of parents and children merely by its connection with the sensual sphere.

On the contrary, quite independent of sensuality, conjugal love in itself constitutes a completely new kind of love. It involves a unique mutual giving of one's self, which is the outstanding characteristic of this type of love.

Conjugal love involves mutual self-giving

It is true that in every kind of love one gives oneself in one way or another, but here the giving is literally complete and ultimate. Not only the heart but the entire personality is given up to the other. When a man and a woman love each other in this way, they give themselves to each other at the very moment they begin to love.

The man wants to belong to the woman, and her to belong to him; and the woman wants to belong to the man, and him to belong to her.

All love certainly desires a reciprocity which is free from every shade of egoism; but in conjugal love there is an aspiration not merely for a return of affection in general, but for the unique love whereby the beloved belongs to the lover in an entirely exclusive manner, as he in turn wants to belong to the beloved.

This love tends to a unique union and even partly constitutes it: a community where two persons constitute a closed union which can exist only between them. Conjugal love establishes a relationship in which the regard of each one of the two parties is turned exclusively upon the other.

Conjugal love: the most profound *I-thou* relationship

Relationships between persons actualize themselves under two profoundly different forms: two persons can be united through a common interest, by facing with each other something extraneous to themselves. Together they may take the same attitude toward a person or thing: they may mourn together and rejoice together, may come to a decision together, and may give thanks together.

This may be called a *we* relationship wherein the partners remain side by side, in which they walk side by side — hand in hand, even.

But two human beings can also turn to face one another, and in touching one another in an interpenetrating glance, give birth to a mysterious fusion of their souls. They become conscious of one another, and making the other the object of his contemplation and responses, each can spiritually immerse himself in the other. This is the *I-thou* relationship, in which the partners are not side by side, but *face to face*.

Of all terrestrial communions, conjugal love is the most pronounced form of an *I-thou* relationship. The beloved person is the object of our thoughts, sentiments, will, hope, and longing. She becomes the center of our life (as far as created goods are concerned). He whose heart is filled with such conjugal love lives not only *with* his beloved but *for* his beloved. Certainly such an *I-thou* relationship in its purest form exists only between the human soul and its heavenly Bridegroom, Jesus. In the last analysis we must live only for Him, and in marriage, too, the two partners live together for Him. But in the realm of created goods, conjugal love means living *for* one another. Compared with all other human relationships, the two partners live in a definite *I-thou* communion.

Conjugal love involves a decision

This giving of self, the specific characteristic of conjugal love (as distinguished from friendship or any other form of love), is also revealed in the decisive character of the words, "I love you." It may not always be easy to say whether someone whom we know well and whom we like very much may at the same time be considered as a friend, and it may be equally difficult sometimes to answer with a simple "yes" or "no" the question whether we like somebody or not. But between love in the conjugal sense and other forms of love there is such a difference that the question whether or not one loves another person in this sense can be answered quite definitely with "yes" or "no."

This love involves a definite decision. By this love we decisively choose a person. The expression "I love you" is characteristic of this decision. To add anything to those words and to say "I love you very much" or "I love you immensely" would be to lessen the force of the statement. Instead of strengthening, it weakens the meaning of the simple declaration, "I love you."

Conjugal love reveals the whole being of the beloved

The fact also that this love can arise quite suddenly, and even develop to maturity at the first encounter of two persons, emphasizes the typical contrast between this and any other kind of love. In this love, the personality of the beloved is instantaneously revealed as a complete unity. Our eyes are able to penetrate the other much more deeply than in the ordinary way when our glance is distracted by innumerable trifling objects and dulled by a grey everyday atmosphere. This never goes beyond the outer aspect. Just as in supernatural love of our neighbor we penetrate at one glance to that inner-most, mysterious essence of the other person in which, through all his imperfections, pettiness, arrogance, and triviality he reflects God, so in natural conjugal love the real individuality of the partner is mysteriously revealed. The deep, secret meaning which permeates all his gifts and talents, the whole rhythm of his being, is disclosed at one glance through all his imperfections. One under-stands, so to speak, the divine plan underlying the cre-ation of this particular *individuality*, just as in love of neighbor one understands the general meaning of a free, spiritual person, created by God after His own image in a particular *individual*.

It is true, of course, that all love implies a deeper understanding of the other person, a deeper grasp of his real being which shines but imperfectly through many veils and weaknesses. Nothing is more mistaken than the adage, "Love is blind." Love is that which *gives us sight*, revealing to us even the faults of the other in their full import and causing us to suffer because of them. But conjugal love reveals to us intuitively the whole being of the other in a mysteriously lucid unity. It not only shows us individual praiseworthy traits but also the particular charm of his individuality as a whole, which permeates everything and characterizes the essence of his being — a charm which can only be completely understood by the complementary person and can have its full significance for him alone.

Conjugal love is possible only between a man and a woman

The special character of conjugal love is, furthermore, marked by the fact that this love can only come into being between men and women and not between persons of the same sex, as is the case with friendship, parental love, or filial love.

It would be quite wrong, however, to reduce this characteristic to the sexual sphere and to say that conjugal love is just friendship plus sexual relations, presupposing a difference of sex. It would be incredibly superficial to consider as a mere biological difference the distinction between man and woman, which really shows us two complementary types of the spiritual person of the human species.

Certainly, man and woman have ultimately but one task, "to be reborn in Christ," and to glorify God by their sanctity. Yet man and woman represent two different

types of mankind, both having their respective significance according to the divine plan, and their special
value quite apart from their procreative function.

Let us take the example of the male and female saints
and consider how they, each in his or her special way,
realized the *unum necessarium*, and how at the same time
they fulfilled ideally the meaning of their respective
natures as men and women. Raising our glance to the
Blessed Virgin, we see that she, who of all creatures is
most like to Christ, could not possibly be imagined as
anything but a woman, and that she, Queen of all
Saints, is womanly in the highest and most sublime
sense of the word.

No: the difference between man and woman is a
metaphysical one. A long time ago the Pythagoreans
divined this when they placed male and female among
the Categories, although in this, of course, they were
not right. The medieval theologians, too, were thinking
of this when they raised the question as to whether or
not the angels were divided into male and female.

At any rate, for the human species this difference
represents two manifestations of the person, analogous
— if this comparison be admissible — to the various
religious orders, which although they are identical in

their aim, represent different ways in the *imitation of Christ*.

These two types, man and woman, have a unique capacity for *complementing* each other. Their meaning for one another is something quite unique. They are made one for the other in a special way, and they can, purely as spiritual persons, form a unity in which they reciprocally complement one another. Marital love — involving the gift of one's own person, whose decisive character is that the partners form a couple, an *I-thou* communion, in which the whole personality of the beloved is grasped mysteriously as a unity in spite of all outer obstacles — can exist only between two types of the spiritual person, the male and the female, as only between them can this complementary character be found.

Being in love is not infatuation

Being in love, which many people consider contemptuously as infatuation, constitutes in itself only the climax of this full spiritual grasping of the beloved person, in which the charm of the other being is completely unfolded, the full bliss of the *I-thou* community realized.

Indeed, being in love is so far from contemptible, so far from being a consequence of the Fall of man, that, within the natural order — as Plato points out admirably in his *Phaedrus* — being in love constitutes the only truly awakened state, a state in which we break the fetters of indolence and cease dragging ourselves dully through life. We become exactly the image of our relation to Christ: "My beloved to me, and I to my beloved, who feedeth among the lilies."[9] Thus, being in love is exalted as a figure of the highest and most sublime relationship to the Son of God.

Conjugal love is not an illusion

Let no one object that it is an illusion, an intoxication which passes quickly and which is based only on the external qualities of the other. For there is a superficial and a deep way of being in love, just as there is superficial and deep friendship.

This general possibility of superficiality does not, however, argue against either *being in love* or against friendship. Nor does the fact that one can be mistaken

[9] Song of Sol. 2:16

prove anything against the revelation of the character of the beloved, which — as we have seen — is implied in the state of being in love. Who would deny that in spite of the fact that in the life of prayer we come to understand much about the soul and its relation to God, self-deception may nevertheless occur?

Love is not sensual desire

Above all, real *being in love*, even in its superficial form, must never be confused with sensual desire. Being in love always implies a respectful, chivalrous attitude toward the beloved — a certain element of humility even, a melting of the soul, of the rigidity of the ego. A person truly in love becomes tender and even pure. Even when this love is a superficial one and only based on the external qualities of the beloved, these qualities, substituting for and representing the beauty and goodness of the entire personality, elevate the soul of the enamored person into a state of mind in which he overcomes his self-centered heaviness and indolence.

Being in love has nothing to do with mere sensual intoxication; neither has it to do with a satanical fascination nor with the sensual captivation of a Don Juan.

Marriage

The intention of duration and strict exclusiveness is one of the implications which lie in the very nature of being in love, as well as of marital love. Anyone who says, "I am in love with this person now but I do not know whether I shall like him later on," is not really in love. Even if in reality one were mistaken and one's love were to pass away later, being in love (like marital love) shows clearly the intention of lasting forever and of strict exclusiveness.

Being in love is an element of conjugal love

We shall return later on to this element of duration and exclusiveness in conjugal love. For the moment, let us point out that being in love also pertains to conjugal love. This does not mean that it has to persist to the same degree as long as conjugal love lasts, but this being in love must be reactualized at specific moments. Implicitly, conjugal love must always bear this potentiality and show this characteristic. The enormous difference which lies between the being in love which constitutes only a climax of this deep conjugal love, and the being in love which appears as an independent phenomenon, need not be pointed out, nor that its normal function

18

consists in representing the full realization of conjugal love.

Conjugal love is so far from being a compound of friendship and sensuality that, on the contrary, its characteristics, which, as described above, distinguish it from all other forms of love, actually serve as the bridge toward the sphere of sexuality and solely make *possible* an organic union of the two. A compound of friendship and sensuality is repugnant. It would be a juxtaposition of heterogeneous elements, and the sensual sphere would in no way be sanctified by a discordant combination of this kind.

Only in conjugal love, where man and woman are united in a unique communion, where they give themselves to one another in the deepest sense of the word and belong to each other in an ultimate interpenetration of their souls, does this relation to the sensual sphere become intelligible. Only in this order can the sublime meaning of the sexual sphere be realized in the union of two beings in a complete spiritual-sensual union according to the words of our Lord and Savior Jesus Christ: "And they shall be two in one flesh."[10]

[10] Matt. 19:5

Polygamy is essentially contrary to conjugal love

Sometimes one comes across the opinion that polygamy is forbidden only by a positive law of God, and that monogamy is not necessarily rooted in the nature of marriage nor demanded by natural morality. Nothing is more erroneous. Not only actual marriage but conjugal love in itself excludes polygamy. Conjugal love in its essence aims at one person only. The characteristics of complete, mutual self-giving, and of being exclusively turned toward the beloved, as well as the fact that the two partners form a couple, exclude in themselves the possibility that this love can be directed simultaneously to more than one person. Having two or more friends is in no way contrary to the principle of friendship and does not constitute something unworthy. But it is not possible for a man to love two women conjugally. The whole value of the relationship would be destroyed. Strictly speaking, it would indeed be impossible.

Conjugal exclusiveness differs from possessiveness

Moreover, to deduce the essential exclusiveness of conjugal love from the general egoistic possessiveness of man would be quite wrong. The owner of a harem who regards his women as mere chattels in his possession does not want anyone else to interfere. This, of course, is pure egoistic possessiveness. But this harem-owner has not the slightest conception of real conjugal love.

Exclusiveness in conjugal love results from the consciousness that this unique love can only exist between *two* beings, at least while this love lasts, and that this wonderful union would be destroyed and torn apart if one partner were to love a second person with conjugal love.

And this exclusiveness concerns the person himself as much as the beloved partner, since one's own infidelity causes one as much horror as the infidelity of the other and is felt just as much as the breach and destruction of the union.

Marriage is more than conjugal love

But conjugal love is not yet marriage, although it contains an anticipation of the meaning of marriage. Marriage is a reality in the objective order which is constituted only by a solemn act and presupposes a formal act of the will: the two partners give themselves expressly to each other, fully sanctioning this surrender for their entire lifetime.

The marriage is fully actualized when both partners, in consequence of this act, consummate this surrender in bodily union. Marriage is a communion of objective validity which includes both partners. Once established, it persists as such, regardless of the sentiments or attitudes of the partners, although it imposes specific obligations on them.

The existence of conjugal love between the partners makes marriage desirable and gives it meaning, but does not in itself establish this objective bond.

For among various human experiences (such as love, respect, or joy) there is one kind which is not merely an inner act in respect to another person, but which also *creates* an objective reality independent of the person. Thus, for example, a promise creates an obligation toward another person and the right of demanding fulfillment by that other person. The command of a superior creates an obligation of fulfillment by the subordinate. Absolution by a priest in the name of God creates the actual annulment of our guiltiness. Certain decisions of the legitimate state authority can become law, and so forth.

Marriage creates an objective bond

In the same way, the act of voluntary surrender of one's own person to another with the intention of forming a permanent and intimate union of love, creates an objective bond which, once established, is withdrawn from the sphere of arbitrary decision of the persons concerned.

We shall see later how this solemn act of marriage attains further an infinitely higher importance and power if it is consciously fulfilled in Christ and if it contains in a way a consecration of both partners to Christ.

The expression *marriage-contract* is not a happy choice of words since marriage differs essentially from any other real contract. Apart from the character of reciprocity, it resembles a contract no more than any promise or any other act of this sort.

The union desired in conjugal love becomes by this act *objectively real in its fullest sense,* and no other earthly communion of love can become objective to such a degree. Both partners now belong wholly to each other. An objective bond unites them: they are no longer *two,* but *one.*

Marriage

Marriage comes about from a free decision

An extraordinary decision is inherent in the act of marriage. Unlike conjugal love, it does not spring into being of itself, but it is a free act like an act of will (in the stricter sense of the term). It marks, as with religious vows, the beginning of a new *status*. An enormous change suddenly takes place. A sublime creation burgeons which, once it flowers, makes the highest demands on the two partners.

Marriage is exclusive and irrevocable

This decisive character of marriage, on the strength of which a change takes place which removes it beyond the range of our influence, also has a qualitative analogy in bodily surrender. The physical union of husband and wife constitutes such an ultimate intimacy between them that of its essence it is a surrender valid once and for all. It is not merely a passing intimacy which establishes no objective relationship. It implies a definite decision of the highest import. It is truly a *surrender* of one's self to the other and implies essentially the same exclusiveness which we found in conjugal love.

From its very meaning and nature, this act can be consummated with but *one* person, for, according to the words of our Lord, "They shall be two in one flesh."[11] It establishes a tie of such infinite tenderness and such deep proximity, so essentially *permanent*, implying such a radical surrender, that it cannot be repeated with another person as long as the person to whom one has given oneself integrally is alive. All these elements are contained in this deepest union.

But this union only becomes a full reality when it follows as a consequence of the solemn conclusion of marriage. How dreadful, therefore, any abuse of this ultimate and most intimate surrender! What a degradation and desecration of the union destined as the ultimate realization of the communion of love which becomes objective through marriage!

Love is the meaning of sexual union

As marriage is, in its nature, principally a communion of love, so the meaning of physical consummation is not restricted to its function as a means of procreation.

[11] Matt. 19:5

Marriage

Certainly, there is no greater mystery in the natural order of things than the fact that this closest of all unions procreates a human being with an immortal soul (although the soul, in each case, is a direct creation of God), and that this act brings a new being into existence destined to love God and to adore Him, a new being made after His image.

But this primary *end* is not the only *meaning* of the physical act. Subjectively speaking, it is not even its primary meaning.

Its *meaning* is primarily the realization of the sublime communion of love in which, according to the words of our Savior, "They shall be two in one flesh."[12] Woman, who according to Genesis was made from the flesh of man (a sign which even then indicated the closeness of their relation and designated her as the inseparable mate of man), is really united to man in this way in marriage.

In contrast to the Protestant and Puritan conception, which even subjectively considers procreation as the sole meaning of the physical union, an old Catholic marriage prayer speaks of marriage as "the mystery of

[12] Matt. 19:5

love." The Methodist Whitefield proudly asserts that love had nothing to do with his courtship, saying, "God be praised, if I know my own heart at all, I am free of this stupid passion the world calls love." But an old Catholic prayer runs as follows, "O God, at the creation of mankind, making woman from man, Thou hast already ordained that there should be a union of the flesh and of sweet love. . . . Lord our God, Thou hast created man pure and immaculate and still Thou wishest that in procreation of the generations one be made from the other by the *mystery of love.*"

Procreation and the communion of love must never deliberately be separated

That a new human being should issue from it is certainly part of the solemn grandeur of this supremely intimate union. The wonderful, divinely-appointed relationship between the mysterious procreation of a new human being and this most intimate communion of love (which by itself alone already has its full importance), illuminates the grandeur and solemnity of this union.

Thus it is that in order to preserve the reverent attitude of the spouses toward the mystery in this union, this general connection between procreation and the communion of love must always be maintained even subjectively, at least as a general possibility of this act.

It is difficult to imagine a greater lack of reverence toward God than interfering with this mystery with desecrating hands in order to frustrate this mystery. How terrible to think of man wanting to destroy this unity which God has established so mysteriously, deeming those united in the highest earthly union of love worthy to take part in His creative power. To go against God's purposes through a desecrating interference, perhaps even thus to throw back into the void a being that God had intended to exist — what sacrilegious presumption!

Childless marriages may nonetheless fulfill the ideal of marriage

Yet if for any reason, beyond the sphere of human influence, it becomes evident that procreation is out of the question, the physical union between man and woman still retains its subjective significance and its intrinsic beauty. Is conjugal love in itself not sublime enough to sanctify and justify this union? Is not the reason for the creation of woman stated in Genesis: "It is not good for man to be alone; let us make him a help like unto himself."[13] Can a childless marriage be regarded as a failure, as something that did not fulfill its meaning? Can we justly assert that it would have been better if such a marriage had not been brought to pass? Can it not have its full, divinely-appointed meaning simply as the highest communion of love, and glorify God by this very fact?

When both partners, even though childless, belong to each other in the most perfect conjugal love, in unchangeable loyalty to one another, in imitation of the union of the soul with God, is not the ideal of marriage fulfilled to an even higher degree than in the case of a marriage with perhaps many children, where the partners are unfaithful to each other and desecrate the sacred tie by a lack of love and loyalty? Need marriage become celibate because of the knowledge that there cannot be any children? Is this not a clear indication that marriage is a symbol of the union of the soul with God, that it possesses, as such, a sublime importance and that it exists in the first place for its own sake and not exclusively for the sake of any result that it produces?

[13] Gen 2:18

Marriage

Every marriage filled with love is fruitful

On closer examination, we see that every intrinsically fulfilled marriage is fruitful even in the deepest sense of the word. The fact that the closest communion of love between two people produces a new human being mysteriously reflects the fruitfulness of love as such.

For we must not forget that every true love possesses an intrinsic spiritual fruitfulness and that conjugal love harbors this spiritual fruitfulness of love quite independently of procreation.

This fruitfulness expresses itself in an *élan* of the soul, which is implied in love, in a new awakening of the soul which stimulates it to spiritual growth and a higher moral life. It expresses itself in the influence which the spouses unconsciously exert on one another, in the spiritual elevation of one another which their mutual understanding makes possible.

Every marriage in which conjugal love is thus realized bears spiritual fruit, becomes *fruitful* — even though there are no children.

He alone can understand the horror of the sin of promiscuity who has grasped the grandeur and sublimity of bodily union as the full realization of conjugal love, and who realizes that besides the primary *end* of procreation, the primary *meaning* of bodily union lies in the fulfillment of conjugal love.

That which is intended to bring two persons together in the highest, most intimate union, to unite them "in one flesh," — the final actual surrender of one's self — is used by the promiscuous as a source of sensual lust and is thereby ignominiously desecrated. And this desecration remains the same whether or not children result from this sinful union.

The words of St. Paul clearly show that the sin of impurity lies essentially in the abuse of the union which God reserved for the closest communion between two people: "Or know you not, that he who is joined to a harlot, is made one body. *For they shall be*, saith he, *two in one flesh.*"[14] Were procreation not only the end but also the *sole meaning* of this union, it would be incomprehensible, in the last analysis, why an illegitimate union should be sinful when children result from it, and a marriage pure and sublime when it serves only the communion of love in a childless marriage.

[14] 1 Cor. 6:16

Only marriage justifies physical union

The justification of this physical union, however, lies not in conjugal love as such, but only in the solemn act of the conclusion of marriage which we mentioned above. Since physical union involves the express and solemn surrender by which one enters into so ultimate and intimate a union with the other person, it presupposes not only the mere existence of conjugal love but also the solemn conclusion of marriage in which one gives oneself freely and irrevocably to the beloved for the entire lifetime.

Love must be nourished in every marriage

As the communion of love represents the deepest meaning of marriage, love is not only a previous condition of marriage but also a sentiment that both partners must make an object of their will, something that has to be protected and cherished. Love is also a task and a duty for both partners. If marriage is the unique projection of this special conjugal love, then marriage, once established, demands love from both partners — not only neighborly love but also conjugal love.

Love and marriage

Each spouse has a right to the love of the other. To maintain conjugal love in its entire grandeur and purity, in its glow, its depth, and its vital plenitude, is a task that arises for both partners with the conclusion of their marriage.

Because our laziness, our dullness, and our constant falling back into the periphery stultifies our vision, it is difficult always to keep before us in all its same clarity and splendor the image of the other person so wonderfully revealed by love. We should and must fight against this dullness, for it constitutes a sin against the temple which we erected in our marriage.

In a certain sense we are already unfaithful to the other when we cease to see him from within, when we understand no longer the deeper character of his being, but regard him as we would regard other people — from the outside.

For those who consider the specific kind of love which we call conjugal as nothing else than an infatuation, it may be natural for this love to fade in the course of time and leave only friendship. We, however, for whom conjugal love includes a deeper understanding of the other, and for whom it is the divinely-appointed relation in marriage, must fight against a weakening of this love, against this *falling asleep*, just as we must always strive — in an incomparably higher sphere — to keep our love for Jesus unfailingly awake.

For someone in a religious order, the fulfillment of the rules of the order represents a continuous effort; so, too, marriage demands abstention from all side issues and deviations which are liable to distract attention from the beloved person and destroy the inner concentration which is implied in love.

But this task differs according to the individual character of the marriage. In the supernatural sphere, God gives mankind grace in different measures and demands more from them according to the measure of grace received. (The Gospel gives us the parable of the talents.) So, too, marriage demands more from the husband and wife in the measure that their marriage as such approaches the ideal, and the more they harmonize as characters.

Love's task in the best of marriages

The greater the love which they felt originally for one another and the greater the love which potentially lies in the nature of the combination of the two persons, the more is mutual love demanded of both. If the combination of two people contains the possibility of this ultimate conjugal love, it becomes the duty of both partners, once the marriage is concluded, to strive toward the realization of this ideal.

They must endeavor to develop this highest love. They must avoid everything that could obscure or mar this love (such as the absorption of the husband in his business affairs or of the wife in household duties). But above all, they must beware of an indolent indifference and of simply floating down the stream of everyday habits. Every hour they must recall anew the unspeakably precious gift which God has given in the form of the soul of the beloved. Never must they lose their sense of the wonderful mystery that the other person whom they love loves them, too, that the other lives for them, and that they own something far above all other earthly possessions.

Love's task in imperfect marriages

If, however, the combination of the two characters of man and wife does not offer the possibility for this conjugal love, if such ultimate inner unity cannot be achieved, the task for both partners becomes a different one. When such is the case, this quality of glowing conjugal love is not demanded of them — for the consorts cannot give this love to one another if it is not preformed by God in the combination of their two characters. Their task here is to attain the highest communion within the limits of the possibilities of their individual case. They, too, must live for one another and avoid everything that could alienate or in any way separate them from one another. They must try to see each other in the highest light.

Love's task in troubled marriages

This holds all the more true for an unhappy marriage. If love is completely lacking on one side, or if one partner suffers from the other in every way — let us remember the marriage of St. Monica — the obligation to live up to the objective tie which the conclusion of marriage has created persists, in spite of the fact that the combination of the two partners does not make possible the realization of ideal conjugal love. The one spouse can only love the other in a particular form of neighborly love — love him because it was with him that the tie of marriage was knit. The task in this special case consists primarily in sacrifice and renunciation and in care for the salvation of the other.

Each marriage has its own particular task

In a word, in each marriage God gives the partners a particular task apart from the obligation *every* marriage contains: mutual love and conjugal faithfulness.

It is, therefore, necessary to understand the particular meaning of each individual marriage, the special call which God makes upon the spouses: the realization of an ideal marriage or the heroic suffering of the cross of an unhappy marriage. The unique, divinely appointed meaning of an individual marriage has to be discovered in each marriage, inasmuch as the task varies according to what appears as the highest attainable possibility in a given combination of two characters.

But this must not mislead us into believing that the objective form of marriage as such does not aim at a subjective fulfillment of a complete union of love, and that all other marriages measured against the divine design of marriage represent failures. Marriage as such does not exist as a trial for the consorts, or to serve as a school of renunciation, but to unite two human beings in boundless love into a complete union and thus, in the most sublime way, to reflect the union between Jesus and the soul.

Love and the mystery of sacramental marriage

For this cause shall a man leave his father and mother
and shall cleave to his wife; and they shall be two
in one flesh. This is a great mystery, but I speak in Christ
and in the Church.
— St. Paul

WE HAVE seen that the primary meaning of marriage — which enables it to serve as an image of the relationship between the soul and God — consists of that closest communion of love whereby two persons become one: one heart, one soul, and one flesh. But what relation does this communion bear toward Jesus, toward the salvation of the soul, and toward the Kingdom of God?

Let us first consider the supernatural significance of sacramental marriage: the transformation of natural marriage that takes place, as well as that which is brought into the Sacrament from natural marriage. Let us also consider the sublime value of marriage and the incomparably high rank it holds above all other earthly communities.

He who was heard by St. John to say: "Behold, I make all things new,"[15] elevated marriage, the noblest

---

[15] Rev. 21:5

41

community of mankind, to unprecedented heights and invested it with sublime dignity.

Sacramental marriage transfigures natural marriage

Great as is this permanent community of love in itself, marriage objectively (as well as subjectively) is even more sublime in Christ and in the Holy Church. Christian marriage — solemnly engaged in for Christ and in Christ, in the light of eternity, and carrying with it a sense of the deepest responsibility — differs radically from even the noblest natural marriage in which one spouse sees the other only within the limits of the natural order.

A world of difference separates the two.

Conjugal love undergoes a deep, even a qualitative change in the living members of the Mystical Body of Christ. Wedded love does not lose the characteristics discussed above: mutual self-giving, the character of an *I-thou* communion, the living for each other, and the formation of a complete unity as a couple closed off from the rest of earthly things.

Indeed, Christian wedded love does not cease in any way to be conjugal love in the full sense of the word. The supernatural does not dissolve this finest earthly good, but rather transfigures it. "The greater the man, the deeper his love," Leonardo da Vinci said. And Lacordaire said: "There are not two loves — an earthly and a divine one. It is one and the same feeling, except that one is infinite."

Conjugal love represents something so great, so ultimate, so vitally enveloping of the whole person, that its depth can be taken as a measure of the depth and greatness of the whole man. It offers the highest and noblest earthly happiness, one which fills the soul more than any other value on earth. It is the noblest of natural powers, moving the world beyond anything else.

Thus the Song of Solomon says, "If a man should give all the substance of his house for love, he shall despise it as nothing."[16]

Christian conjugal love sees the beloved as an image of God

This conjugal love is, of course, fully preserved in Christian marriage. But in Christian marriage, conjugal

[16] Song of Sol. 8:7

love assumes a completely new depth. It achieves a completely new seriousness, purity, and unselfishness in those persons who see everything consciously in the sight of God, who are aware that all things acquire an authentic importance only in Jesus and through Jesus, and who consider their own sanctification and that of others for the glory of God as the primordial, true task of man. Conjugal love is here based on sublime Christian charity.

This is not to say that conjugal love does not represent something completely new in relation to the love of our neighbor and that it must not conserve its specific nature.

Rather, love in Christian marriage is fully aware that the beloved is a being created by God — even more, an image of God and, indeed, an immortal soul redeemed by the blood of Jesus and loved by Jesus with an infinite and eternal love.

The whole individual charm and the particular atmosphere of the beloved which touches in a unique way the soul of the consort — these are incomparably ennobled when they appear as a particular aspect of the eternal value of the spiritual person who has become a temple of the Holy Spirit.

Christianity deepens and intensifies conjugal love

So long as we do not conceive of the person as an image of God, as an immortal soul destined to eternal communion with God — above all, so long as we do not consider the person as a vessel of grace, we have not grasped the authentic dignity and ultimate solemnity which is invested in the beloved and which is connected with the destiny, depth, and beauty which this person is called upon to fulfill.

How greatly is conjugal love increased and deepened when we recognize in the beloved a member of the Mystical Body of Christ, belonging to Christ as we ourselves belong to Him. What respect and chastity must permeate conjugal love which is aware of this mystery! What sublime rhythm, far beyond that of even the most ardent and noble natural love, must penetrate it!

We see here the sense in which the conjugal love of the Christian also embraces the supernatural love of our neighbor.

In this way, conjugal love in its entirety is deeply transformed. It acquires a new and extraordinary solemnity, an unexpected depth, for in loving the partner we love Christ simultaneously. *In* the beloved, we love Christ.

Christian conjugal love desires
the eternal welfare of the beloved

By this fact, conjugal love assumes also a character of purity and unselfishness not to be found even in the highest natural love. Conjugal love, like every authentic love, implies a genuine intention to make the beloved happy. He who loves is even more anxious for the happiness of his beloved than for his own. The lover lives in the beloved, seeks the happiness of the beloved, and not the enjoyment of his own love.

But in supernaturally transfigured conjugal love, this intention is elevated to a fervent desire for the *eternal* welfare of the beloved. The eternal welfare of the beloved is not only desired in the same way as the salvation of our neighbor in general, but with the particular consciousness that this is the person destined for me, whose salvation concerns me in a particular way and above all others. Collaboration in the sanctification of the beloved becomes the focus of our love, raising it gloriously above the life of this world. It embraces the beloved not only within the limits of this life and for this life, but also for eternity. The eternal welfare of the beloved is the culminating point of all that his love affirms. This lends to this love a touching selflessness which is not possessed even by the highest natural love.

Christian conjugal love avoids idolatry of the beloved

Further, natural conjugal love exposes us to the danger of making the beloved the absolute center of our life. This love can degenerate into idolatry. In supernatural conjugal love, this danger is banished. It consciously builds itself in the love of the King and Center of all hearts. The ultimate *logos* of this love is participation in that eternal love which Jesus holds for the soul of the beloved.

Nor will it be any the less ardent for this, any less directed toward the beloved. On the contrary, it acquires an ardor and ultimateness which the merely natural-minded cannot even imagine. For abandonment to a good is deepest and strongest when the good is viewed in the exact order ordained by God. Far from being a superabundance of love, any idolatry is rather a perversion, and therefore a diminution of love.

Marriage

The spiritual fertility of Christian conjugal love

As we have seen before, conjugal love possesses, as does every authentic love, an intrinsic spiritual fertility which, although mysteriously connected with procreation, is by no means restricted to it. The impulse to *lift up our hearts* which characterizes conjugal love does not allow the lovers to become completely absorbed in one another, but generates in both a movement of spiritual ascension. The lovers let themselves be transported upward by their love. A primordial concern for the perfection of the partner arises in their souls.

Authentic, deep love always erects a sanctuary, harboring both lovers but arching high above them. A deeper and deeper penetration into this sanctuary is part of the intrinsic movement of love.

The supernatural transfiguration of conjugal love gives a new significance to its spiritual fruitfulness. Jesus Himself erects the sanctuary of this love, and true love in Christ impels each consort to lead the other toward Jesus. Not only is true love filled with an insatiable longing to see the beloved more and more transformed into Christ, not only does it join in the divine love of Jesus for the sake of the other, but it actually fosters this transformation, as, in its turn, the love of the beloved lifts the lover himself to the heights.

Marriage attains its full dignity only in Christ

Even more important than the transformation of conjugal love is the transformation of marriage, a transformation which also retroactively affects conjugal love, as we shall see later on. Great as is the natural tie originated by the solemn conclusion of marriage, which expresses the will to belong to one another in a permanent communion, nevertheless the decision consciously realized in God creates here a tie of an infinitely higher dignity and reality. An oath carries much greater weight than a mere assurance and, as an invocation of the name of God, engenders a much more serious and solemn obligation. Similarly, marriage in Christ attains a greater dignity and reality. Indeed, only in the marriage fulfilled in God does the objectivity and validity immanently inherent in every marriage find its full achievement. Here alone is achieved the full realization of the unity and communion of love in an existence which is independent of the changing dispositions and feelings of either consort. This communion alone represents in itself a good for which both partners must strive and make sacrifices. Here alone does marriage become a reality that does not exist exclusively for the consorts, but something for which the consorts themselves exist.

Christian marriage is a form of consecration to God

Christian marriage embraces even more than all this. Not only is it concluded in God, but the partners' promise of mutual fidelity is also a promise made to Christ.

This solemn union is not only contracted with the spouse; it also concerns Christ to whom both partners belong as members of His Mystical Body. The conclusion of marriage, therefore, becomes a consecration to God which may be likened to a religious vow. It does not only mean that both spouses give themselves to each other in God; they give themselves anew to Christ in the other.

The sacred tie is placed in the hands of Christ, is confided to Him. The marriage bond belongs to Him. To unfold this bond in its ideal form, to cherish it as a sublime community of love, to protect it as a sanctuary from every profanation, is a *divine service*.

Christian marriage is essentially related to God

This must not be understood only in the broad sense (as, for instance, the sense in which professional work, when it is expressly consecrated to God, can be called *divine service*) but in a much more radical sense, analogous to the religious state, although in a much lower degree.

For the nature of marriage as such, through its glorification of God in a unique objectification of love, carries a much deeper relation to Him and is in a specific way formally rooted in God *because* it is something solemnly concluded in Christ. Finally, our Lord and Savior Jesus Christ has established the relation of marriage to Himself, thus connecting it in a unique manner intimately with God.

The higher a good and the more directly it is connected with God by its own nature, the more it glorifies God directly. Thus, all that concerns the ideal development of marriage becomes a divine service in a stricter sense than does a professional work which is not directly and by its nature related to the reign of God.

The fact that marriage has been solemnly concluded in Christ and confided to Him in its whole content establishes a much more intimate and more organic link with God than that which issues from a simple act of offering something to God. Finally, not only is it connected with God through certain specific acts of ours, but Christ Himself expressly establishes this connection.

As the objective bond of marriage is thus connected in a threefold way with God and belongs not only to the consorts but also to Christ, all loving acts — the fulfillment of the vocation which lies in marriage and the actualization of its meaning as an ultimate community of love — become a divine service in a stricter and more radical sense than professional work performed with the intention of glorifying God. Marriage in Christ thus surpasses by far the way in which all things — even the most insignificant — can and must be related to God, according to the words of St. Paul: "Therefore, whether you eat or drink, or whatsoever else you do, do all to the glory of God."[17]

The bond of a Christian marriage thus becomes something sacred, comparable to the religious state which originates in the taking of vows — although, as

[17] 1 Cor. 10:31

we shall see later on, the religious state surpasses marriage by far in its sacred character.

Sacramental marriage is a source of grace

But Jesus has invested marriage with a dignity which represents something quite new in reference to all that we have considered until now. He raised it to the rank of a Sacrament. He made of this sacred bond a specific source of grace. He transformed marriage — already sacred in itself — into something *sanctifying*. In this respect marriage even surpasses the religious state, although the latter surpasses it by far in respect to intrinsic holiness, as we have just pointed out.

Sacramentally, marriage is like Holy Orders

With regard to its sacramental character, marriage must be compared to Holy Orders. Leaving aside the internal holiness of the functions implied in the idea of a priest (which of its very nature calls down meriting graces), the priesthood — in its character as a Sacrament — is a source of specific graces, a dispenser of graces. The same applies to marriage.

Holy Orders not only carries graces with it, but produces grace and is the channel of special graces. In the same way, marriage has been honored in becoming one of the seven mysterious sources of participation in divine life.

Perhaps marriage as a Sacrament shows the closest affinity to Holy Orders, since it does not effect a rebirth (as do the Sacraments of Baptism and Penance) nor a perfection of this rebirth and a union with Christ (as does the Sacrament of the Eucharist). Like Holy Orders, the Sacrament of Matrimony is at the disposal only of certain people who receive a special vocation for it.

Its sacramental character has been incorporated into the essence of marriage

It is not our task to develop further this purely theological part of our problem, and I shall stress only one point. The sacramental character has been incorporated in a specific way into the essence of marriage. It does not originate in the priest's blessing but issues from the decision of the two partners. The consorts are themselves the ministers of this Sacrament. The fact that the Sacrament is actualized through mutual consent to that union (which is an image of the union of Christ and His Church), and that in the administration of the Sacrament both spouses act with respect to one another, reveals in an admirable manner the primary meaning of marriage as a communion of love.

Another specific characteristic of marriage is the incorporation of the Sacrament into the matter of marriage. That the sacramental character in this case has been placed in marriage itself and connected so intimately with its inherent holiness is a further proof of the high value of marriage.

The indissolubility of marriage presupposes the existence of God

We have seen above how duration and exclusiveness are implied in the very intention of conjugal love, how marriage represents a community into which one enters freely but which, once established, can no longer be arbitrarily dissolved. This validity, which is beyond the reach of the arbitrary decision of the spouses, presupposes necessarily the existence of God and the eternal destiny of man, although it does not necessarily presuppose a subjective reference to God in the conclusion of marriage. If we were to conceive the world merely as a mechanism not ruled by an almighty and infinitely good God, a world in which our being ceases completely with death, then an objectivity which is beyond the arbitrary decision of the spouses would be nonsense.

Once the existence of God is admitted, the marriage bond is immediately placed beyond the arbitrary decision of the consorts, even if they do not refer themselves subjectively to God.

Therefore, no real marriage (even among pagans) can be dissolved according to the whim of the partners. But that its indissolubility is not absolute is proved by the Pauline privilege. Only sacramental marriage as an image of the union of Christ and the Church possesses that full validity and reality which make it absolutely indissoluble.

Sacramental marriage is the perfection of marriage

However, the indissolubility of sacramental marriage is not merely the result of a positive law of God which is essentially unconnected with the nature of marriage. One should rather say that in sacramental marriage, marriage finds the perfection of its sublime meaning.

The element of decision which the conclusion of marriage in itself implies, and which, as we saw above, is also included in the unique character of the physical union, finds its full development and reality in the bond which is concluded in Christ, confided in Christ, and which represents His union with the Church. For the Savior reestablished this strict indissolubility when He referred to the original state in Paradise with the sublime words, "What God has joined together, let no man put asunder."[18]

The indissolubility of marriage arises from its intrinsic sublimity

There are few things in our Holy Church which cause as many conflicts, as many desertions and apostasies, as does the dogma of the indissolubility of marriage. It sometimes demands the greatest of sacrifices: the renunciation of a happy marriage by those who are unhappily married. How ridiculous and paltry it would be if, instead of searching for the reason for the indissolubility of marriage in its intrinsic sublimity, we were to

[18] Matt. 19:6

suppose that something which has such decisive consequences was commanded by God merely for some secondary reason, as for instance, the role that marriage plays within the state or society — to say nothing of some biological consideration. It is superficial to fail to see that the radical indissolubility of marriage flows from its nature as an intimate communion of love, and to attempt to deduce this indissolubility from such utilitarian considerations as the prevention of the decay of society, the safeguarding of the education of children, and so on. All these are considerations which pertain only indirectly to indissolubility.

It would be just as if one were to give the reason for the indelibility of the priesthood (its character *indelebilis*) by saying that this is necessary in order to strengthen the trust of the faithful in the priest, instead of searching for the reason in the very nature of priesthood and in its inherent sublimity.

No.

Christian marriage, according to its meaning as the most intimate created community of love, is by its nature so sublime and so closely connected with Christ that even if the union is an unhappy one, it remains indissoluble.

Conjugal love seeks the indissolubility of marriage

The indissolubility of marriage has an important retroactive effect on conjugal love. It is considered by many as something oppressive and dispiriting, something which deprives love of its wings and gives it a coercive character. They think that love would vanish with the knowledge that the tie is binding whether love persists or not. But nothing is less true. For the real lover, the consciousness of being indissolubly united with his beloved in Christ, of forming an objectively indissoluble community whose validity is beyond all wavering and all human frailties, is a source of the highest satisfaction. For he wants to be one with his beloved, and he is grateful and happy that this unity can be realized to so great a degree and that it rises above all emotional changes.

Irrevocable self-giving fulfills conjugal love

Conjugal love implies an intention of *going beyond* even the giving of self, which is inherent in love as such. It desires an objective self-giving once and for ever, an irrevocable giving which persists independently of all subjective inconstancy. Here we touch the intrinsic superabundance of this love, the heroic element proper to it. A similar superabundant love impels certain persons to give themselves once and for ever exclusively to God. Thus they desire to bind themselves by eternal vows in order to effectuate this self-bestowal objectively and irrevocably, which, once established, is independent in its validity of all our wishes and feelings. Such persons experience the possibility of an irrevocable self-giving as the specific fulfillment of their love.

The indissolubility of marriage must likewise be considered as the unique fulfillment of the specific intention of conjugal love. The true lover experiences the objective validity of his self-bestowal, and the accomplishment of such a transcendent, irrevocable decision, as a specific fulfillment of his love.

Conjugal love requires an heroic spirit

Certainly this decision involves a great risk; and when the choice of the spouse happens to be based on an illusion, the indissolubility of marriage may prove a great cross for one or both consorts. But it lies in the nature of conjugal love to be bold, heroic, not to shrink back from taking a risk. *All great things on earth are connected with risk.* Without risk, human life — *in statu viae* — would be deprived of all grandeur and heroism. Do not religious vows imply a similar risk? If the vocation proves itself as an illusion, the religious state can become a heavy cross, a burden hard to bear. Yet an heroic love of God is willing to take such a risk, even desires to take it.

Marriage is not a bourgeois affair, a kind of insurance for happiness, providing a way of escape from every eventual cross. Does not every love as such carry with it a great risk of suffering? In attaching our hearts to a person, do we not run the risk of enduring terrible sufferings, through misfortunes that may happen to our beloved or separation from her when she dies? Should we then abstain from love in order to prevent the possibility of great sorrow?

He whose life is dominated by the intention of avoiding any possible cross excludes everything that gives human life grandeur and depth. He will never know real abandon — never know real, deep happiness. Remaining in a mediocre self-centeredness, he will never be able to do anything without a certain reserve; he will always provide for a possibility of retreat.

All life is overshadowed by death: *"Media in vita mortis sumus."* We must never forget that we do not live in Paradise, but that as a consequence of the Fall of man, we live in a world which is permeated by a deeply tragic element, where happiness is necessarily wrapped up with tribulation.

The redemption of the world by our Lord has not suspended disharmony and banished suffering, although He gave a new meaning to suffering by making it a means of penance and sacrifice. He transfigured it by the Holy Cross behind which shine the rays of eternal harmony.

Thus, in this fleeting, earthbound life all that is great and important is connected with risk, and calls for a holy boldness, an heroic spirit of unconditional abandon. The law of all great things *in statu viae* is expressed in the words of our Lord: "No man putting his hand to the plough, and looking back, is fit for the Kingdom of God."[19]

Of course all great decisions, insofar as they carry with them great risks, should be deeply considered before we undertake them. Entering into marriage calls

[19] Luke 9:62

for a full realization of the great and decisive step which it represents, and requires profound self-examination. The objective form of marriage must correspond to the deepest meaning of marriage as the most perfect and intimate union of love, and cannot be conformed to the case of a failure.

Against this background the unspeakable shabbiness and stupidity of a trial marriage clearly appears. Trial marriage is in itself contradictory to the nature of conjugal love. Anyone who even considers trial marriage has never experienced conjugal love.

Marriage is the most intimate communion of love in Jesus and for Jesus, a community which belongs to Jesus and brings about the sanctification of both spouses. In it, two persons are one in one flesh and have been allowed to participate in the creation of a new human being by God. This community has been elevated to a Sacrament as an image of the union of Christ and the Church.

Mutual love is the proper motive for marriage

Once we fully realize the grandeur and mysterious sublimity of Christian marriage, the question of the proper motive for entering marriage assumes great importance. Only one motive can be admitted as completely adequate for marriage: *mutual love and the conviction that this union will lead to the eternal welfare of both spouses*.

Just as faith in divine truth permeated by love is the sole ultimate and true motive for conversion, so, too, the conviction that this is the person whom God has destined for me, and that I am the person destined for her, and that God has joined us both in conjugal love, is the only motive which can make this community desirable and give it meaning.

Only the existence of such a love, the authenticity of which must first be well examined and proved, should form the decisive reason for marrying.

Although, as we have seen, the married couple have a motive for love in the fact that they are conjugally united (even the bare fact of their conjugal union demands this love), still the ultimate motive for their love should be found in the qualities of the other's personality.

Conjugal love does not exist only to serve marriage (to make marriage easier or to make it possible, so that one might be prompted to love someone because one already wishes to marry him). No: marriage is there as a fulfillment of conjugal love. We should marry someone because we love this person destined for us by God.

Other motives are sometimes permissible

Although love is the real and adequate motive for concluding a marriage, this does not mean that all other motives are morally unworthy. A love implying a certain renunciation may also justify the entrance into marriage. By this, we mean a love which is not based on this unique, gladdening interpenetration of souls, this conviction of being destined for each other, but which is penetrated by a deep esteem for the partner and animated by the intention of forming a noble community of life.

Conjugal love in the plenitude of its perfection is not granted to every man. For instance, we may never meet the person who fully corresponds to us, and the conclusion of a marriage animated only by a love with a certain resignation attached to it cannot be considered as morally inadmissible, although it is certainly not a situation in which the real meaning of marriage can fully unfold itself.

Marriage

Many people also are too coarse, too blunt, too primitive to experience such an ultimate conjugal love. They may, nevertheless, marry — although they only experience a more superficial love.

Unworthy or reprehensible motives for marriage

A merely sensual desire without any authentic love must, on the contrary, be considered as a completely inadmissible motive. This selfish and external relation, which degrades the other person to something impersonal, is in direct contradiction to the sublime meaning of a communion completely uniting two persons until death separates them. It is a kind of sacrilege to conclude this solemn bond whose meaning is the most personal union of love, for so superficial, temporary, and base a motive.

Interest in economic advantages or any kind of ambition (such as the desire to participate in the worldly position of the partner or to bear his name and share his influence) — indeed, all motives not concerned with the other person as such are completely unworthy.

Obviously it would be shameful for a person to enter a religious community in order to be secure for the rest of his life, when he had not succeeded in finding any position in the world. In the same way, it would be shameful to form a bond in which two persons become one by mutual love in Jesus for the sake of an exterior advantage.

This does not mean that a marriage concluded for morally inadmissible motives cannot later on become a true community of love which glorifies God, just as it is possible that someone who enters a religious order for unacceptable motives may become later on a good religious. But this subsequent development by no means justifies the unworthiness of the motives.

Only a marriage motivated by love is reasonable

Unfortunately, it seems that these inadmissible motives are not always sufficiently condemned by Catholics. One must be implacably clear in rejecting them as completely unworthy and must insist that conjugal love alone should constitute the authentic motive for marriage. Even in Catholic circles we often find the disastrous concept of a *reasonable marriage*. By this is meant a marriage which issues not from so-called *sentiment* but from rational considerations.

This implies a wrong alternative. Obviously, the decision to marry someone should also be a subject of examination by our intellect — but the precise subject of that intellectual examination should be the question of whether the conjugal love (which is here rather contemptuously treated as sentiment) really exists between both persons, whether the prospective spouse is really what she seems to be, whether she is the person whom God destined for me, whether the projected union is something pleasing to God, and whether there is any danger in this union for her eternal welfare or for mine.

But as soon as the intellect turns to matters not relevant to marriage or to matters of secondary importance, or — even worse — makes these considerations in themselves the motive of marriage, it misses completely its proper role, which is to consider and clarify that preexisting love which is the proper motive for marriage. How could we refer to a marriage of this kind as other than *unreasonable?* To be reasonable, an attitude must be in conformity with the nature and meaning of the thing to which it is referred.

To enter a religious order is a reasonable action when it is the response to a real call from God and when the existence of a vocation has been intently examined. But when intellectual considerations regarding the utility of monastic life for some selfish purpose serve as a substitute for a vocation, the motivation contradicts the meaning of monastic life. However soberly considered the decision may be, the motivation is thoroughly unreasonable.

A so-called *marriage of reason* (which is decided after a cold calculation that one's financial situation can be improved and certain professional advantages attained, or that both are peaceful and will get on together, or that their ages are well suited) — a marriage where such considerations (rather than conjugal love) constitute the motivation, where there is no longing for an indissoluble community with the beloved, is not only deprived of all beauty and plenitude, but is also something definitely *unreasonable*.

Marriage is the highest of human communities

We have sketched briefly the transformation and transfiguration of natural marriage by the Sacrament of Matrimony. We must still briefly examine the specific value of sacramental marriage.

Every community of love has its specific value. A value is inherent not only in the love of the lovers, but also in the union of love in which both persons are united: "Behold how good and how pleasant it is for brethren to dwell together in unity."[20] The deeper and more central this union of love, the greater is the value of this community. Now, as we have seen, the most intimate community of love among persons is marriage. Thus, even as a merely natural community, it surpasses any other (such as the family, state, or nation). It glorifies God more than these.

In its value, marriage ranks far above all other earthly communities. The higher the good which forms its intrinsic principle, the higher a community ranks. Further, the deeper the point in the soul to which the union appeals, the greater and more essential the role which love plays in it finally, and the more closely the unifying principle is connected to our supernatural destiny, the higher the community is. A social club, for example, ranks below the nation. For the high cultural good which is the unifying principle of the nation ranks much higher than the promotion of superficial amusements

[20] Ps. 133:1

which might form the purpose of a social club. The unifying principle in a nation is obviously rooted much more deeply in the person, and mutual love assumes a more prominent role in this community.

But a community infinitely higher than the nation is the family. That which unites the members of a family appeals to a much deeper point in the person than the national element. Its unifying principle surpasses by far the realm of culture and reaches into the metaphysical order. Mutual love here plays an intrinsic role. The fulfillment of this community involves this love to a much higher degree, and that which pertains to its perfection is much more closely connected with the supernatural than in the case of a nation or a state.

But the community of marriage is even superior to the community of the family itself. The unifying principle here touches the deepest roots of personal life. Here, as we saw before, love is the essence of the relationship. Its principle embraces not only the most intimate happiness of each but also the mutual abandon of love, an ardent interest in the spiritual and moral growth of the beloved, an affirmation of the unique idea of God which is incarnated in the other person. This community involves the person in his whole nature as does no other community. It extends to all spheres of life, from the most central to the peripheral. That is why its nature is so exclusive.

In marriage as a community brought to fruition in Christ and, above all, in marriage as a Sacrament, the focus of the principle becomes the attempt to imitate the love of Christ for the Church. *Burning interest in the eternal welfare of the beloved* is the supreme intention of our love. Marriage thus has an infinitely more direct relation to Jesus and to our eternal destiny than does any other earthly community.

Marriage is greater than the nation or the state

It is characteristic of the pagan errors of our epoch to believe that the nation and state rank higher than the family and higher even than marriage, and, above all, to consider interest in the nation or in the state as something more unselfish than the surrender of self to the family or to the marriage relationship. These communities are believed superior only because they are numerically vaster and have a longer life than marriage.

In reality they are much inferior. The most perfect state or nation cannot glorify God as much as a perfect marriage. Let us never forget the only decisive question which is always in all things: "What is for the greater glory of God?"

Marriage is also more free of egoism because it is primarily not a *we* community but an *I-thou* community. In marriage, the authentic antithesis of egoism results not from the consciousness of a *whole* of which I am a part, but from the love of neighbor, whom I face as a *thou*.

We cannot dwell any further on this important question beyond seeing the rank that marriage holds among communities and understanding that it represents in itself something far superior to all others, and that in itself it would glorify God as an image of the relationship of Christ and His Church even if no other communities existed.

Christian marriage directly glorifies God

Christ our Lord told us: "Where two or three are gathered together in my name, there am I in the midst of them."[21] What sublime value lies in the heart of

[21] Matt. 18:19

Marriage

Christian marriage, where two human beings not only unite themselves in lifting up their eyes to Christ, but also form in Christ an ultimate unity, the very existence of which glorifies the Savior. What sublime value is inherent in this touching, luminous, chaste conjugal love which makes both spouses feel, so to speak, in one and the same pulsation of their souls, but *one* sorrow, *one* pain, *one* joy, and *one* love of Jesus! What beauty is possessed by this tie, a bond which requires of us this conjugal love and implies a task which is an image of our eternal end — the union of the soul with God!

Let us think of St. Elizabeth, who, passing the night in prayer, left her hand in the hand of her sleeping husband — a touching expression at once of authentic, ardent conjugal love and of sacred union, fully penetrated by reverence *in conspectu Dei*. Does not a community such as this glorify God in a specifically direct and primary manner?

Sacramental marriage quickens love of Jesus

Let us add that Christian marriage also represents for both consorts a way to attain an ever-increasing union with Jesus. As the bond has been concluded in Jesus and toward Jesus, the increase of conjugal love also means a growth in the love of Jesus. The unique abandonment to the beloved, the life of love which one lives and should live, opens the heart and enables it to love more and more. In a conjugal love outside of Christ, spouses run the risk of erecting a wall between themselves and God; here, however, their conjugal love itself becomes a source for their progression in the love of Christ.

Yet consecrated virginity is superior to marriage

Precisely for this reason, virginity consecrated to God is incomparably superior to marriage. Its superiority does not follow from a lack of conjugal love for a spouse, but from the fact that instead of the reference of conjugal love to Jesus, there is in this virginity marriage with Jesus Himself.

Marriage with Christ is the authentic end for every soul, and this can be achieved notwithstanding an earthly marriage. But virginity consecrated to God actualizes this nuptial marriage within its own status.

This state is more sublime because one consciously offers to Jesus the great sacrifice of the noblest earthly good, and above all, because one directly achieves the status of marriage with Christ.

In itself, the celibate state possesses no superiority over marriage, but rather an inferiority. Only virginity which has consciously been chosen for the reign of God and consecrated to God — either in a religious order or in the world — constitutes a superior state, because it implies a formal, nuptial wedding with Christ, because here a greater love is demanded over against the state of human marriage. In virginity, God does not call us to a stoic ideal of apathy, but to fill our hearts with the most intense and vital love.

Woe to those in this superior status, who, instead of becoming more ardent and more sensitive, are affected by a certain hardheartedness which removes them further from God than they originally approached Him by their renunciation.

No: the virginal state is infinitely superior to marriage because it demands more love; because in order to be perfect, the state of virginity, far from being the *grave* of our hearts, requires the greatest depth of feeling, a supernaturally transfigured plenitude of love.

In a word, the Catholic conception of the superiority of the state of virginity reveals that it is exclusively its greater love which constitutes its excellence in the eyes of God. If, therefore, we are to grasp the profound meaning and value of marriage, we must never forget the sublime words of our Lord: "I am come to cast fire on the earth, and what will I, but that it be kindled?"[22]

[22] Luke 12:49

Biographical note
Dietrich von Hildebrand (1889-1977)

H ITLER feared him and the late Pope Pius XII called him "the twentieth-century Doctor of the Church." For more than six decades, Dietrich von Hildebrand — philosopher, spiritual writer, and anti-Nazi crusader — led philosophical, religious, and political groups, lectured throughout Europe and the Americas, and published more than thirty books and many more articles. His influence was widespread and endures to this day.

Although von Hildebrand was a deep and original thinker on subjects ranging across the spectrum of human interests, nonetheless, in his lectures and writings, he instinctively avoided extravagant speculations and convoluted theories. Instead, he sought to illuminate the nature and significance of seemingly "everyday" elements of human existence that are easily misunderstood and too frequently taken for granted.

Therefore, much of von Hildebrand's philosophy concerns the human person, the person's interior ethical and affective life, and the relations that should exist between the person and the world in which he finds himself.

Von Hildebrand's background made him uniquely qualified to examine these topics. He was born in beautiful Florence in 1889, the son of the renowned German sculptor, Adolf von Hildebrand. At the time, the von Hildebrand home was a center of art and culture, visited by the greatest European artists and musicians of the day. Young Dietrich's early acquaintance with these vibrant, creative people intensified his natural zest for life.

In Florence, von Hildebrand was surrounded by beauty — the overwhelming natural beauty of the Florentine countryside and the rich beauty of the many art treasures that are Florence's Renaissance heritage. Pervading this Florentine atmosphere was Catholicism: in the art, in the architecture, and in the daily life of the people. These early years in Florence quickened in von Hildebrand a passionate love of truth, of goodness, of beauty, and of Christianity.

As he grew older, he developed a deep love for philosophy, studying under some of the greatest of the early twentieth-century German philosophers, including Edmund Husserl, Max Scheler, and Adolf Reinach.

Converting to Catholicism in 1914, von Hildebrand taught philosophy for many years at the University of Munich.

However, soon after the end of World War I, Nazism began to threaten von Hildebrand's beloved southern Germany. With his characteristic clearsightedness, von Hildebrand immediately discerned its intrinsic evil. From its earliest days, he vociferously denounced Nazism in articles and speeches throughout Germany and the rest of Europe.

Declaring himself unwilling to continue to live in a country ruled by a criminal, von Hildebrand regretfully left his native Germany for Austria, where he continued teaching philosophy (now at the University of Vienna) and fought the Nazis with even greater vigor, founding and then publishing for a number of years a prominent anti-Nazi newspaper, *Christliche Ständestaat*.

This angered both Heinrich Himmler and Adolf Hitler, who were determined to silence von Hildebrand and to close his anti-Nazi newspaper. Orders were given to have von Hildebrand assassinated in Austria. However, von Hildebrand evaded the hit-squads and, thanks to his Swiss passport, was finally able to flee the country just as it fell to the Nazis.

Marriage

It is characteristic of von Hildebrand that even while he was engaged in this dangerous life-and-death struggle against the Nazis, he maintained his deep spiritual life, and managed to write during this period his greatest work, the sublime and highly-acclaimed spiritual classic, *Transformation in Christ*.

Fleeing from Austria, von Hildebrand was pursued through many countries, ultimately arriving on the shores of America in 1940 by way of France, Spain, Portugal, and Brazil.

Penniless in New York after his heroic struggle against the Nazis, von Hildebrand was hired as professor of philosophy at Fordham University where he taught until his retirement. Many of his best works were written during this period and after his retirement. He died in 1977 in New Rochelle, New York.

Dietrich von Hildebrand was remarkable for his keen intellect, his profound originality, his prodigious output, his great personal courage, his deep spirituality, and his intense love of truth, goodness, and beauty. These rare qualities made Dietrich von Hildebrand one of the greatest philosophers and one of the wisest men of the twentieth century.

Sophia Institute Press

S OPHIA Institute is a non-profit institution that seeks to restore man's knowledge of eternal truth, including man's knowledge of his own nature, his relation to other persons, and his relation to God.

Sophia Institute Press serves this end in a number of ways. It publishes translations of foreign works to make them accessible for the first time to English-speaking readers. It brings back into print many books that have long been out of print. And it publishes important new books that fulfill the ideals of Sophia Institute. These books afford readers a rich source of the enduring wisdom of mankind.

Sophia Institute Press makes high-quality books available to the general public by using advanced, cost-effective technology and by soliciting donations to subsidize general publishing costs.

Your generosity can help us provide the public with editions of works containing the enduring wisdom of the ages. Please send your tax-deductible contribution to the address noted below. Your questions, comments, and suggestions are also welcome.

For your free catalog, call:
Toll-free: 1-800-888-9344

or write:

Sophia Institute Press
Box 5284
Manchester, NH 03108

Sophia Institute is a tax-exempt institution
as defined by the Internal Revenue Code, Section 501(c)(3).
Tax I.D. 22-2548708